WHEAT BELLY COOKBOOK FOR WEIGHT LOSS

25 GRAIN FREE RECIPES FOR YOUR SLOW COOKER

CHARLOTTE MOYER

TABLE OF CONTENTS

Welcome

Introduction

25 Grain Free Slow Cooker Recipes

- Duck Curry
- Chicken Soup
- Perfect Pork Ribs
- Mediterranean Vegetable Bake
- Slow Cooked Lamb in a Fruit Sauce
- Spiced Apples
- Duck in a Date Sauce
- Mixed Bean Stew
- Slow Cooked Chili Con Carne
- Slow Cooked Prawn Curry
- Oriental Barbecued Pork
- Indian Coconut Curry
- Rustic French Chicken
- Traditional Apple Sauce
- Cajun & Thyme Jambalaya
- Ginger & Cinnamon Fruit Chutney
- Wheat-Belly Gratin

- Alcoholic Ginger Brew
- Caramelized Apple Juice
- Bacon & Collard Greens in a Vinaigrette
- Stuffed Peppers with Goats Cheese & Italian Sausage
- Rosemary, Garlic & Ricotta Cheese Dip
- Hot Caribbean Soup
- Greek-style Roast Turkey
- Meat feast Casserole

Conclusion

About the author

Other Books By Author

- Wheat Belly: 21 Day Wheat-Free Plan, full of Quick & Nutritious Recipes
- Wheat Belly: 31 Delicious Wheat Free Recipes to Lose Weight Fast
- How to Bake Perfectly: 101 Tips, Tricks & Cheats for Baking Recipes
- How to Make Money from Home: 7 Steps to Make Money from Baking recipes

Welcome

Thank you for purchasing this book, *Wheat Belly Cookbook for Weight Loss: 25 Grain Free Recipes for Your Slow Cooker*. The wheat belly diet advocates an eating pattern that avoids wheat, most grains and other types of carbohydrates.

Although these restrictions still allow a whole wealth of foods and meals to be made, many people will have to learn a new repertoire of meals from scratch. Fortunately, this book provides 25 recipes that you can use whilst sticking to the wheat belly regime.

The recipes in this book cover a wide range of main courses and meat dishes. In addition, this book covers a range of stews and vegetables bakes. There is also a selection of sweet slow cooked foods; caramelized drinks and other delicacies. All recipes have the nutritional information of the resulting meal or beverage provided for your convenience; you can use this to order your meal plan or count your calories (if you desire!).

Enjoy the following recipes and the inevitable weight and health benefits of the wheat belly diet.

Introduction

According to the principles of the wheat-belly diet, wheat is our enemy. Wheat is demonized for its hurtful impact on our digestive system, causing us to feel bloated, develop allergic symptoms, cause constipation or diarrhea and damage gastro-intestinal health.

However, it is not only just wheat that is detrimental to our health but most other types of grains and staple carbohydrates; including rice, barley and potatoes. These carbohydrates (as well as several others) are metabolized quickly, causing havoc with our energy levels and blood sugar. The result is lingering and persistent fatigue, potentially serious complications arising from poor blood sugar management and weight gain.

The wheat belly diet advocates a new, healthier pattern of eating; cut out the wheat and other grains. This leads to a diet high in vegetables, meat, fish, nuts, seeds, pulses, oils and fats. The wheat belly diet is reported by most to cause weight loss as well as increase meal satiation and avoid all the troubling symptoms of wheat.

Unfortunately, most people are not equipped with the knowledge to eat a diet without wheat or other common carbohydrates. Wheat and others grains are ubiquitous in western society and the western diet. Almost every processed product and every meal you eat will have some quantities of these undesirable substances within.

This book provides 25 wheat belly recipes to help get you over the entrance hurdle to the wheat belly diet. In particular, this book provides slow cooker wheat belly recipes. Slow cooker recipes are fantastic for individuals aiming to diet and change their eating patterns. Slow cooking naturally infuses and embeds food with a huge amount of flavor, combating the tendency for diet meals to feel bland and dull. Furthermore, slow cooker meals also tend to be relatively easy to make and besides the cooking duration, take almost no time to prepare.

This helps you stay disciplined and focused in your eating habits – it prevents you from sticking to the wheat belly diet out of laziness or time concerns. In fact, it is common amongst the slow cooker community to prepare meals in the morning so that you alleviate the need to prepare a main meal during the evening.

Within this recipe list, there are some ingredients, used on occasion that are less than ideal for the wheat belly diet. In particular, many of the beverages are especially high in sugar.

Ensure that when you make these recipes, you stick to the portion sizes, consume these beverages rarely and eat them alongside a meal. The wheat-belly diet is not an ultimatum; it does not dictate that you never eat simple carbohydrates again. However, the wheat belly diet does ask you to be wiser in your habits. Use the higher sugar recipes as they are intended; occasional treats. You still have a wealth of other, hearty wheat belly recipes to enjoy, everyday without guilt.

Bearing this in mind, use the following wheat belly slow cooker recipes can help you in leading a healthier, happier lifestyle.

DUCK CURRY

Total Preparation Time:

Approx. 2 hours & 30 minutes

Ingredients (serves 6):

6 duck legs

2tablespoons of light brown sugar

4 tablespoons of red Thai curry paste

2 tablespoons of fish sauce

1 pineapple

1 red chili

Basil leaves

Nutritional Information:

660 calories

38g protein

20g carbohydrates

49g fat

20g saturates

2g fiber

18g sugar

2.3g salt

Procedure:

Preheat the oven to 350F or gas mark 4. In a frying pan, fry the duck legs for 15 minutes or until browned on all sides. Do not add any oil. Removing the duck legs, combine the brown sugar with the fat residue left in the pan. Once the mixture has caramelized, add the curry paste and continue to fry for 2-3 minutes. Next add the coconut milk, also adding half a cup of water. Stir the mixture thoroughly and simmer for 5 minutes. Finally, combine the fish sauce and lime leaves into the mixture to complete the curry sauce.

Pour the curry sauce over the duck legs and slow cook for 90 minutes or until the duck meat is soft and breaks easily.

Meanwhile, peel and dice the pineapple. Using the previous frying pan, briefly fry the pineapple in the leftover sauce for 2-3 minutes. Add extra chili and basil leaves if desired whilst frying. Put the pineapple aside and serve with the duck curry when ready.

Chicken Soup

Total Preparation Time:

Approx 1 hour

Ingredients (serves 4):

1 tablespoon olive oil

2 onions

3 carrots

1 tablespoon chopped thyme

1.5litres of chicken stock

300g roast chicken (leftovers or bought prepared)

200g frozen peas

3 tablespoons of Greek yogurt

1 garlic clove

Lemon juice

Nutritional Information:

339 calories

39g protein

18g carbohydrates

13g fat

3g saturates

6g fiber

11g sugar

2g salt

Procedure:

Peel and dice the onions. Peel the carrots and chop them into medium slice. Crush the garlic clove. In a frying pan, heat the olive oil and fry the onions, carrots and chopped thyme for 15 minutes. Add the fried vegetables with the chicken stock in your slow cooker. Leave the mixture to simmer on a low heat for 30 minutes.

Tear and break the roast chicken into small segments. Drop the chicken into the frying pan and stir. Separate half the slow cooker mixture by pouring it in a large bowl. Next, using a hand blender, blend the mixture remaining in the slow cooker until pureed.

Add the non-pureed mixture back to the slow cooker along with the frozen peas and a pinch of salt. Heat until the entirety of the soup is warm.

Combine the Greek yogurt with the crush garlic and a dash of lemon juice. When ready to serve, briefly mix the yogurt sauce into the soup.

Perfect Pork Ribs

Total Preparation Time:

Approx 9 hours

Ingredients (serves 4):

1 ½ kg of pork ribs

350g of barbecue sauce

2 pork stock cubes

2 bay leaves

1 teaspoon of coriander seed

1 teaspoon of mustard seed

1 teaspoon of peppercorn

Nutritional Information:

420 calories

23g protein

25g carbohydrate

24g fat

7g saturates

1.5g fiber

21g sugar

2g salt

Procedure:

Place four tablespoons of your chosen barbecue sauce in your slow cooker with all the other ingredients. Add extra water to ensure that the pork ribs are submerged in liquid. Slow cook for around 8 hours and 30 minutes.

30 minutes before serving, preheat your oven to 425F or gas mark 7. Remove the ribs from the slow cooker gently; the meat will be incredibly soft and may break apart if handled without finesse. Coat the ribs using the leftover barbecue sauce. Place on a baking tray and cover with tin foil. Cook for 25 minutes or until the rib skin has become crisp. Serve when ready.

Mediterranean Vegetable Bake

<u>Total Preparation Time:</u>

Approx 7 hours

<u>Ingredients (serves 6):</u>

4 garlic cloves

400g chopped tomatoes

Oregano

Chili flakes

300g eggplant

2 zucchinis

½ jar of roasted red peppers

3 beefsteak tomatoes

Torn basil

250g mozzarella balls

Nutritional Information:

275 calories

14g protein

31g carbohydrates

10g fat

6g saturates

4g fiber

8g sugar

1g salt

Procedure:

Place your slow onto a high setting. Crush three garlic cloves and add these to your slow cooker alongside the chopped tomatoes, a pinch of chili flakes, oregano and salt. Cover these ingredients and leave to slow cook for several moments.

Chop the eggplant, zucchini, red peppers and beefsteak tomatoes into moderate sized slices. Remove the tomato sauce from the slow cooker. Take your vegetable slices and place half of them in layers in your slow cooker. Cover these layers in half your tomato sauce, a pinch of chili, oregano and half your mozzarella. Repeat once more for the remaining ingredients. Cover and slow cook for 6 hours and 30 minutes. Serve with salad or a side of your choice.

Slow Cooked Lamb in a Fruit Sauce

Total Preparation Time:

Approx. 3 hours and 20 minutes

Ingredients (serves 2):

4 teaspoons of olive oil

2 lamb shanks

3 onions

4 garlic cloves

½ cinnamon stick

1 tablespoon of cumin

1 tablespoon of crushed coriander seeds

Chili flakes

400g chopped tomatoes

500g chicken stock

2 tablespoon of pomegranate molasses

4 dried apricots

4 dried figs

Fresh, chopped coriander

Nutritional Information:

1120 calories

95g protein

64g carbohydrates

55g fat

23g saturates

10g fiber

52g sugar

2g salt

Procedure:

Preheat your oven to 350F or gas mark 4. In a casserole dish, coat your lamb shanks with 2 teaspoons of olive oil. Cook your lamb shanks for 3-5 minutes on each side. Remove from the oven and leave.

Chop the garlic cloves into thin slices. Peel and slice the onions. In a frying pan, heat two teaspoons of olive oil and fry the garlic and onions for 10 minutes or until golden and tender. Add a pinch of chili flakes, cumin and the crushed coriander seeds and fry for an additional 5 minutes.

Remove the sauce from the frying pan and pour it into your slow cooker. Add your lamb shanks, chicken stock and chopped tomatoes. Turn your slow cooker onto a medium setting, cover and cook for 2 hours, ensuring to turn the lamb shanks periodically.

Chop the apricots and figs. Add the apricots, figs, and coriander and pomegranate molasses to the slow cooker and cook for another 30 minutes. Remove the lamb shanks from the slow cooker, cover them in tin foil and gently heat in an oven dish to keep warm. Meanwhile, continue to slow cook and reduce the sauce until it is dense and sticky. Finally, cover your lamb shanks in the sauce and serve with a side of your choice.

Spiced Apples

Total Preparation Time:

Approx. 2 hours and 45 minutes

Ingredients (serves 4):

4 red apples

80g brown sugar

45g unsalted butter

2 tablespoons of pecans, finely chopped

2 tablespoons of raisins

¾ teaspoon of ground ginger

80ml water

A dash of cream

Nutritional Information:

470 calories

3g protein

20g carbohydrates

31g fat

18g saturates

7g fiber

13g sugar

0g salt

Procedure:

Core the apples using an apple corer, ensuring that the bottom of the apple remains attached. With a spoon pry away some more of the apple flesh so there is a sizable hole in the middle of each apple. Using a sharp knife, score the skin of each apple several times.

Chop the pecans and the raisins into small pieces. Add the pecans, sugar, butter, raisins and ginger into a mixing bowl and stir. Divide this mixture into four portions and fill the space created in the apples with this mixture.

Place your apples in your slow cooker. Add enough water to the slow cooker so that your apples are almost, but not entirely, submerged. Bake on a high temperature for 2 hours and 30 minutes. Serve each apple with a dash of cream.

Duck in a Date Sauce

Total Preparation Time:

Approx. 5 hours & 45 minutes

Ingredients (serves 6):

2 teaspoons sunflower oil

6 duck legs (skinned)

2 garlic cloves

1 red chili

2 inch ginger stem

1 tablespoon of cumin

1 tablespoon of coriander

1 tablespoon of cinnamon

1 teaspoon of ground ginger

2 lemons

200g dates

400ml passata

100g almonds

Fresh mint

Nutritional Information:

527 calories

53g protein

30f carbohydrates

20g fat

3g saturates

5g fiber

27g sugar

0.5g salt

Procedure:

In a frying pan, warm the sunflower oil and fry the dugs legs until golden brown all over, one at a time. Next, turn your slow cooker to a low heat and place the duck legs within.

Dice the onion. Cut the lemons into halves, removing the pulp and pith. Using a food processor, blend the onion, garlic, chili, ginger and the lemon skin into a paste. Next, in the frying pan that was used to brown the duck legs, fry the paste for 5 minutes or until soft. Remove and set aside.

Place the dates into the food processor with 1 cup of water. Process until another paste is formed.

Scoop the date paste into the slow cooker with the duck legs and pour in the lemon seasoning. Finally, pour the passata into the slow cooker and stir thoroughly. Slow cook the duck legs in sauce for at least 5 hours. Garnish with chopped almonds and serve with a side of your choice.

Mixed Bean Stew

Total Preparation Time:

Approx 2 hours

Ingredients (serves 4):

8 chipolatas

800g mixed beans

800g chopped tomatoes

1 teaspoon of basil

2 teaspoon of oregano

1 tablespoon of sugar

1 tablespoon sunflower oil

Nutritional Information:

335 calories

20g protein

37g carbohydrates

15g fat

5g saturates

10g fiber

13g sugar

2.7g salt

Procedure:

Heat the sunflower oil in a frying pan and fry the chipolatas for 5 minutes or until each sausage has browned on both sides. Turn your slow cooker to a low setting and place the chipolatas within. Add in the chopped tomatoes, mixed beans as well as the oregano, basil and sugar. Leave to slow cook for 2 hours and serve.

Slow Cooked Chili Con Carne

Total Preparation Time:

Approx 1 hour & 45 minutes

Ingredients (serves 4):

2 tablespoons of olive oil

2 onions

3 garlic cloves

2 tablespoons of chili powder

2 teaspoon of cumin

2 teaspoon of oregano

1kg lean minced beef

2 beef stock cubes

2 large red peppers

10 sundried tomatoes

1200g kidney beans

Nutritional Information:

820 calories

75g protein

59 carbohydrates

35g fat

12g saturates

16g fiber

21g sugar

5g salt

Procedure:

Peel and dice the onions and chop the garlic in fine pieces. In a large frying pan heat a tablespoon of the olive oil and fry the onions for 5 minutes or until soft and golden. Add the garlic, oregano, cumin and chili powder and fry for an additional 2 minutes. Next, add the mince to the frying pan, frying for 15 minutes or until the mince is browned all over. Add the chopped tomatoes, as well as the stock cubes and ½ a cup of water. Stir thoroughly and leave to simmer for 5 minutes.

Turn your slow cooker on to a low setting and transfer your frying pan mixture to your slow cooker. Cover and leave to cook for 30 minutes.

Dice and de-seed the peppers. Add the peppers and sun dried tomatoes to the slow cooker and cook for an additional 30 minutes.

Finally, add the kidney beans to the slow cooker and cook for an additional 20 minutes.

Separate into four portions and serve with a side of your choice.

Slow Cooked Prawn Curry

Total Preparation Time:

2 hours & 30 minutes

Ingredients (serves 4):

1 tablespoon of vegetable oil

2 onions

6 tomatoes

Large piece of fresh root ginger

6 garlic cloves

3 tablespoons curry paste

400g shelled raw king prawns

250g frozen peas

Coriander

Nutritional Information:

235 calories

24g protein

18g carbohydrates

0g fat

1g saturates

6g fiber

10g sugar

1.2g salt

<u>Procedure:</u>

Peel the onions. Cut the onions in half and slice each onion half into six even-sized wedges. Cut each of the tomatoes into eight wedges. Peel the ginger and chop it into small pieces. Finally, cut the garlic cloves into moderate sized chunks.

In a frying pan, heat the vegetable oil and fry the onions for 5 minutes or until soft and golden. Remove the onion from the pan and process with the tomatoes and ginger in a food processor, leaving ¼ of the tomatoes for later usage.

Fry the remaining tomatoes with the curry paste for 5 minutes. Add the prawns and fry until the prawns are thoroughly cooked. Transfer the content of the frying pan and food processor to your slow cooker. Turn your slow cooker to a low setting, add the peas and coriander to the mix and stir. Cover and slow cook for 2 hours. Separate into four portions and serve.

Oriental Barbecued Pork

Total Preparation Time:

Approx. 8 hours & 30 minutes.

Ingredients (serves 8):

¼ cup of soy sauce

¼ cup of hoisin sauce

3 tablespoons of ketchup

3 tablespoons of honey

2 garlic cloves

Small piece of fresh ginger

1 teaspoon of sesame oil

½ teaspoon of five-spice mix

1 boneless pork shoulder, fat trimmed

250ml chicken broth

Nutritional Information:

227 calories

21.6g protein

12.7g carbohydrates

9.5g fat

3.1g saturates

0.5g fiber

9g sugar

0.6g salt

Procedure:

Crush the garlic. Peel and grate the ginger. Combine the soy sauce, hoisin sauce, ketchup, honey, crushed garlic, sesame oil and five spice powder in a bowl. Stir thoroughly. Transfer the spice sauce to a seal-able plastic bag. Add the pork to the plastic bag, and then shake the bag and leave to marinate for 2 hours.

Next, place your slow cooker onto a low setting. Empty your pork and spice sauce into the slow cooker. Cover and leave for 8 hours.

Finally, add the chicken broth and slow cook for another 30 minutes. Tear the pork into shreds and serve alongside the sauce.

INDIAN COCONUT CURRY

Total Preparation Time:

Approx. 6 hours & 30 minutes

Ingredients (serves 6):

1 tablespoon olive oil

2 onions

3 carrots

1 tablespoon curry powder

1 teaspoon brown sugar

Small piece of fresh ginger

2 garlic cloves

1 serrano chili

800g chickpeas

400g chopped tomatoes

500ml vegetable broth

1 green bell pepper

A pinch of salt

A pinch of ground red pepper

¼ teaspoon black pepper

3 cups baby spinach

1 cup coconut milk

2 lemons

Nutritional Information:

276 calories

10.9g protein

44.7g carbohydrates

7.2g fat

1.9g saturates

10.6g fiber

0g sugar

0.6g salt

Procedure:

Peel and dice the onions. Crush the garlic. Peel and chop the carrots into moderate sized pieces. Peel the ginger and cut it into fine pieces. Heat the olive oil in a frying and add the onions and carrots. Fry for 5 minutes, or until the vegetables are soft and the onion golden. Add the brown sugar, curry powder, ginger, garlic and chili frying for another 2-3 minutes.

Transfer the frying pan contents into the slow cooker. Add all the other ingredients except the baby spinach, coconut milk and lemons, then stir. Turn the slow cooker onto high heat, cover and leave to cook for 6 hours.

Next, add the coconut milk and spinach. Slow cook for another 15 minutes. Separate into six portions and serve with a slice or two of lemon.

Rustic French Chicken

Total Preparation Time:

Approx 8 hours and 15 minutes

Ingredients (serves 4):

4 chicken breast halves, skinned

2 teaspoons dried basil

A pinch of salt

A pinch of black pepper

1 yellow bell pepper

400g cannellini beans

400g chopped tomatoes

Nutritional Information:

281 calories

44.9g protein

18g carbohydrates

2.2g fat

0.5g saturates

5g fiber

0g sugar

0.5g salt

Procedure:

Dice the pepper. Turn your slow cooker to a low setting and place all the ingredients in a slow cooker. Cover and leave for 8 hours, then separate into four portions and serve.

Traditional Apple Sauce

Total Preparation Time:

Approx. 12 hours

Ingredients (serves 4):

1 cup brown sugar

½ cup of honey

¼ cup apple cider

1 tablespoon ground cinnamon

¼ teaspoon ground cloves

A pinch of ground mace

10 apples

Nutritional Information:

132 calories

0g protein

35.3g carbohydrates

0g fat

0g saturates

3.1g fiber

35.3g sugar

>0.05g salt

Procedure:

Peel the apples and chop them into large pieces. Combine the apples, spices, cider, honey and brown sugar in a slow cooker and stir. Place the slow cooker on a low heat and cook for 10 hours.

Remove the mixture from a slow cooker. Strain the sauce through a sieve; apply pressure to any apple pieces with a spoon to extract all the juice. Remove and discard any remaining apple pulp or flesh. Return the sauce to the slow cooker and cook on low for 1 ½ hours, stirring every 10 minutes. Use as a topping for fruit and sweet treats.

Cajun & Thyme Jambalaya

Total Preparation Time:

Approx. 6 hours & 30 minutes

Ingredients (serves 8):

2 onions

1 large celery stalk

250ml of water

½ teaspoon of Cajun seasoning

½ teaspoon Dried thyme

225g andouille sausage

450g boneless chicken thighs

400g chopped tomatoes

450g of shrimp

Nutritional Information:

315 calories

30g protein

28g carbohydrates

8.5g fat

3g saturates

10.6g fiber

0g sugar

0.4g salt

Procedure:

Peel and dice the onions. Chop the celery into moderate sized chunks. Dice the chicken thighs into large chunks. Peel and devein the shrimps. Add all ingredients except for the shrimp into a slow cooker. Turn the slow cooker to a low setting, cover and leave to cook for 6 hours.

Next, add the shrimp to the slow cooker. Cook for another 15 minutes. Separate into eight portions and serve with a salad.

Ginger & Cinnamon Fruit Chutney

Total Preparation Time:

Approx. 5 hours & 15 minutes

Ingredients (serves 4):

1 tablespoon sunflower oil

2 onions

6 peaches

200g golden raisins

200g brown sugar

50g crystallized ginger

1 teaspoon of mustard seeds

½ ground ginger

¼ teaspoon of ground cinnamon

¼ teaspoon of ground cloves

450g almond meal

100ml cider vinegar

Nutritional Information:

245 calories

11.4g protein

29.3g carbohydrates

6.5g fat

5.2g saturates

4g fiber

29.3g sugar

0.6g salt

Procedure:

Peel and dice the onion. Slice the peaches into medium sized chunks. In a frying pan heat the sunflower oil and fry the onion for 5 minutes or until soft and golden brown.

Add the onion and all other ingredients, except the vinegar and almond meal, into a slow cooker and set aside for one moment.

Combine the almond meal and cider vinegar in a bowl, whisking until thoroughly blended. Add this mixture to the slow cooker. Turn the slow cooker on to a low setting, cover and cook for 5 hours. Store in a jar or plastic container and serve with cheese, meat dishes or curries.

WHEAT-BELLY GRATIN

Total Preparation Time:

Ingredients (serves 12):

1 tablespoon of butter

1 cup of sweet onion

1 tablespoon almond flour

1 teaspoon chopped fresh thyme

900g sweet potatoes

½ teaspoon kosher salt

½ of a teaspoon ground black pepper

900g

Fresh parmesan

250ml vegetable broth

Nutritional Information:

90 calories

3.4g protein

13.8g carbohydrates

2.5g fat

1.3g saturates

2.2g fiber

0g sugar

0.2g salt

Procedure:

Chop the sweet onion into thin slices. Peel and thinly slice the sweet potato. Heat the sunflower oil in a frying pan and fry the onion for 5 minutes, or until soft and golden brown.

Next add the onion to a mixing bowl with the sweet potato, almond meal, thyme, kosher salt, black pepper and half of the parmesan. Mix to coat all the ingredients with the almond meal.

Spray your slow cooker with cooking spray. Transfer the almond flour-coated ingredients to the slow cooker. Add in the vegetable broth and break in the remaining parmesan. Turn the slow cooker on to a low heat, cover and cook for 4 hours.

Separate into 12 portions and serve with a salad or side of your choice.

Alcoholic Ginger Brew

Total Preparation Time:

Approx 4 hours & 15 minutes

Ingredients (serves 14):

8 cups of water

10 lemons

2 cups of honey

5 tablespoons of crystallized ginger

Large piece of fresh ginger

¾ cup of rum

¾ cup of brandy

Nutritional Information:

226 calories

0g protein

45.6g carbohydrates

0g fat

0g saturates

0g fiber

45.6g sugar

>0.05g salt

Procedure:

Chop the crystallized ginger into fine pieces. Peel the fresh ginger and chop the ginger stem into ¼ inch thick slices.

Place all ingredients, except for the rum and brandy, into a slow cooker. Turn the slow cooker on to a high setting, cover and cook for 4 hours.

Remove the brew, discarding the ginger strips. Add the brandy and rum then stir. Serve in a punch bowl or pouring jug.

Caramelized Apple Juice

Total Preparation Time:

Ingredients (serves 12):

125g sugar

3 tablespoons of water

1 tablespoon of butter

A dash of whipping cream

5 allspice berries

5 whole cloves

2 medium sized cinnamon sticks

10 cups of apple cider

¼ cup of orange juice

1 tablespoon of lemon juice

Nutritional Information:

180 calories

1g protein

38.4g carbohydrates

3g fat

1.9g saturates

10.6g fiber

0g sugar

>0.05g salt

Procedure:

In a saucepan, combine the water and sugar. Heat for 2-3 minutes until the sugar melts. Continue to heat for another 5 minutes or until the mixture is golden. Do not stir as this will crystallize the caramel.

Take the saucepan away from the heat and leave to stand for 1 minute. Stir in the tablespoon of butter and then add a generous dash of cream. Return the saucepan to the heat, until the mixture is thoroughly combined, smooth and warm.

Place the spices in a layer of cheesecloth, tying the edges of the cheesecloth in a knot so that the spices cannot escape.

Add the cheesecloth bundle, caramel sauce, cider and orange juice to the slow cooker. Turn the slow cooker on to a low setting, cover and cook for 3 hours. Serve and stir in a dash of lemon juice.

Bacon & Collard Greens in a Vinaigrette

Total Preparation Time:

Approx. 4 hours & 20 minutes.

Ingredients (serves 5):

1 tablespoon of sunflower oil

3 slices of bacon

1 onion

450g fresh collard greens

A pinch of salt

2 garlic cloves

1 bay leaf

400ml of chicken broth

3 tablespoons of balsamic vinegar

1 tablespoon of honey

Nutritional Information:

82 calories

10.9g protein

13.6g carbohydrates

1.8g fat

0.8g saturates

3.8g fiber

2g sugar

0.3g salt

Procedure:

Peel and dice the onion. Chop the collard greens in small leaves. Crush the garlic.

In a frying pan, heat the sunflower oil and fry the bacon until crisp on both sides. Using a fork, break the bacon into small pieces. Add the onions, frying for 5 minutes or until the onion is soft and golden. Add the collard greens, frying for another 3 minutes.

Transfer the frying pan contents to a slow cooker. Add in the garlic, bay leaf, chicken broth and a pinch of salt, then stir. Turn the slow cooker on to a low setting, cover and cook for 4 hours.

Mix the honey and balsamic vinegar in a bowl. Separate the slow cooker contents into five portions and serve, decorating with the honey-vinegar garnish.

Stuffed Peppers with Goats Cheese & Italian Sausage

<u>Total Preparation Time:</u>

Approx 4 hours & 15 minutes

<u>Ingredients (serves 4):</u>

¾ of a cup of water

½ of a cup of couscous

125g Italian Sausage

A pinch of kosher salt

¼ teaspoon of ground black pepper

200g garlic goat cheese

4 red bell peppers

2 tablespoons of fresh basil

<u>Nutritional Information:</u>

300 calories

18g protein

28.8g carbohydrates

12.7g fat

5.5g saturates

4.6g fiber

0g sugar

0.6g salt

Procedure:

In a saucepan, boil the water. Add the couscous and remove from the heat. Leave aside for 5 minutes.

Add the sunflower oil to a frying pan, and fry the sausages for 5 minutes or until brown on both sides. Tear the sausage into pieces then combine with the couscous. Add the kosher salt and pepper, as well as ¾ of the goat's cheese then stir.

Cut the bell pepper tops of from the main pepper body. Set the tops to one side; you will use them later. Remove any seeds and white flesh from inside the pepper. Stuff the peppers with the sausage, couscous and cheese mixture and rest the pepper tops on the peppers. Place in a slow cooker. Turn the slow cooker on to a low setting, cover and cook for 4 hours.

Serve the peppers with the remaining cheese and salad.

Rosemary, Garlic & Ricotta Cheese Dip

Total Preparation Time:

Approx 2 hours & 15 minutes

Ingredients (serves 15):

¼ of a cup of olive oil

6 garlic cloves

800g cannellini beans

1/3 of a cup of water

150g fat-free ricotta cheese

100g parmesan cheese

1 teaspoon rosemary

¼ of a teaspoon of black pepper

½ teaspoon of grated lemon rind

100g pitted olives

Nutritional Information:

130 calories

7.5g protein

11g carbohydrates

6g fat

1.5g saturates

2.7g fiber

0g sugar

0.6g salt

Procedure:

Slice the garlic cloves into small pieces. Heat a tablespoon of olive oil in a frying pan then fry the garlic for 5 minutes, or until golden brown.

Next, add the garlic into a food processor alongside the water, the remaining olive oil, cannellini beans, ricotta cheese, parmesan cheese, rosemary and black pepper. Blend until a smooth paste is formed.

Transfer this paste to a slow cooker. Turn the slow cooker onto a low heat, cover and then cook for 2 hours.

Pit and chop the olives into small chunks. Stir the olives into the dip and serve with carrots, celery or other ingredients to dip.

Hot Caribbean Soup

Total Preparation Time:

Approx 8 hours & 30 minutes

Ingredients (serves 8):

1 tablespoon olive oil

1 red onion

1 green bell pepper

1 red bell pepper

1 jalapeno pepper

1 garlic head

¼ a cup of tomato paste

800ml of vegetable broth

1 teaspoon dried thyme

½ teaspoon of ground ginger

½ teaspoon of allspice

¼ teaspoon of red pepper

A pinch of salt

800g black beans

½ a cup of coconut milk

½ a cup of fresh cilantro

2 limes

Nutritional Information:

143 calories

5.5g protein

20.5g carbohydrates

5g fat

3g saturates

5.6g fiber

0g sugar

0.3g salt

Procedure:

Peel and dice the red onion. Dice and deseed the peppers and slice the jalapeno pepper into small strips. Crush each clove of the garlic head.

Heat the tablespoon of olive oil in a frying pan, then add the onion and jalapeno pepper, frying for 5 minutes or until the onion is soft and golden brown.

Next, add the garlic and fry for another 2-3 minutes. Add the tomato paste as well as ¼ of the vegetable broth, and then stir. Transfer the contents of the frying pan into a slow cooker. Add all the remaining ingredients, bar the black beans, coconut milk, cilantro and limes. Turn the slow cooker on to a low heat, cover and cook for 8 hours.

Finally, add the coconut milk and stir. Serve each portion with a garnish of cilantro and a slice or two of lime.

Greek-style Roast Turkey

Total Preparation Time:

Approx 7 hours & 30 minutes

Ingredients (serves 8):

1 large onion

100g pitted olives

½ of a cup of sun-dried tomato halves

2 tablespoons of lemon juice

2 garlic cloves

1 teaspoon of Greek seasoning

½ of a teaspoon salt

A pinch of black pepper

1 boneless turkey breast

125ml of chicken broth

3 tablespoons of almond meal

Thyme sprigs

Nutritional Information:

315 calories

57g protein

7g carbohydrates

4.9g fat

0.9g saturates

10.6g fiber

0g sugar

0.5g salt

Procedure:

Peel and dice the onion. Crush the garlic cloves. Add all the ingredients, except 50ml of chicken broth and the almond meal, to a slow cooker. Turn the slow cooker on to a low heat, cover and cook for 7 hours.

Whisk the almond meal and remaining chicken broth together until blended, then add to the slow cooker and stir. Cover and cook for another 30 minutes. Serve the turkey in slices with a side.

Meat feast Casserole

Total Preparation Time:

Approx. 5 hours & 15 minutes

Ingredients (serves 8):

1 tablespoon of sunflower oil

2 slices of bacon

2 onions

1 teaspoon of dried thyme

½ teaspoon of dried rosemary

3 garlic cloves

½ teaspoon of salt

½ teaspoon of black pepper

800g chopped tomatoes

800g Great Northern Beans

1 pound boneless pork loin roast, fat trimmed

½ pound of smoked sausage

8 teaspoons of fresh, grated parmesan

8 teaspoons of fresh parsley

Nutritional Information:

249 calories

22.2g protein

24g carbohydrates

7.6g fat

2.7g saturates

4.6g fiber

0g sugar

0.6g salt

Procedure:

Peel and dice the onions. Crush the garlic. Dice the pork into large chunks and slice the sausage into moderate chunks.

Heat the sunflower oil in a frying pan. Fry the bacon slices until crisp on both sides, then tear apart with a fork. Add the diced onion, rosemary, garlic and fry for another 3 minutes. Add the chopped tomatoes, salt, pepper then stir. Leave to simmer for 5 minutes.

Take half the Great Northern beans and mash them into a paste. Add the remaining beans, sausage and pork and then stir.

Add the tomato sauce and bean-meat sausage mix to a slow cooker in alternate layers. Turn the slow cooker onto a low heat, cover and cook for 5 hours. Serve with parmesan cheese and parsley.

Conclusion

We all want to be healthy. Most of us probably want to lose weight too. It is also far too common for people to complain of various, preventable health maladies such as bloating, fatigue and digestion problems.

The wheat belly diet allows you to become healthier, shed a few pounds and exorcise those lingering, persistent health problems that don't seem to go away. If you are one of those people who cannot seem to get a grip on your health and weight than the wheat belly diet is the solution.

This book has provided you with 25 wheat belly slow cooker recipes to aid you in your quest for better health and weight loss. You know now how to cook sumptuous slow cooked meat dishes with all your favorites; pork, duck, bacon, sausage, chicken and more.

You are now also acquainted with how to create spicy, aromatic and enticing stews using pulses and vegetables. You can make wheat belly friendly meals inspired by the Mediterranean, the oriental east, the Caribbean, and Western Europe.

You even know how to make yourself an occasional sweet treat, using fruits and the secrets of cinnamon, ginger and allspice. You should never find yourself lacking a drink to warm yourself during winter or to celebrate an occasion.

Above and beyond all of this, you also know have 25 meals with nutritional information to use for whatever meal plan you should desire. You are informed and equipped with all the tools and techniques you need to be a successful wheat belly dieter.

About the Author

I am a mother to three beautiful children and a wife to a wonderful husband. I have a passion to teach others and can often be found volunteering in my local community.

During college I worked within my family catering business to support myself. After graduating I opened a chain of small cafes that I ran successfully for a number of years. Now whilst being a stay at home mom, I am able share my skills, knowledge and experience through my books. I feel a great deal of satisfaction when helping others and seeing them flourish to their maximum potential.

Please check out my author page on Amazon to see my latest publications. Please don't forget to **Download your free gift 'Drop the Fat' ebook**.

Once again I want to thank you for reading my book. I really hope you got a lot out of it.

If you enjoyed this book I would really appreciate it if you could leave me a positive review on Amazon. You can **click here** to go directly to the book on Amazon and leave your review.

I love getting feedback from my readers and reviews on Amazon really do make a difference. I read all my reviews and would really appreciate your thoughts.

Thanks so much.

CHARLOTTE MOYER

Other Books By Author

Grab Your Free Gift

Drop the Fat Now!
Natural Solutions to Getting Trim

>>Click Here To Download "Drop the Fat Now" for

FREE<<

Wheat Belly: 21 Day Wheat-Free Plan, full of Quick & Nutritious Recipes

WHEAT BELLY: 31 DELICIOUS WHEAT FREE RECIPES TO LOSE WEIGHT FAST

Vegan: 35 High Protein Vegan Recipes for Weight Loss and Building Muscle

HOW TO BAKE PERFECTLY: 101 TIPS, TRICKS & CHEATS FOR BAKING RECIPES

How to Make Money from Home: 7 Steps to Make Money from Baking Recipes

46022314R00049

Made in the USA
Middletown, DE
20 July 2017